FLAGS

Martin Gitlin

Rourke
Educational Media

rourkeeducationalmedia.com

State flags tell big stories in small spaces. A tiny star might deliver a powerful message. Flags have served as inspiring symbols of heritage for more than 100 years. But their histories extend far beyond that.

The seeds were planted during the Revolutionary War (1775–1783). That is when American colonies designed flags for their armies. State flags maintained a military purpose through the Civil War (1861–1865).

But national celebrations later that century motivated states to show off their pride through symbols. The result was that 19 of 45 states boasted their own official flags by 1901. They have been fluttering in front of state capitol buildings ever since.

Designers faced no easy task. They sought to capture the legacy and greatness of their states in a rectangle a few feet long and wide. They looked to create flags that would inspire love and passion for the states they represented. They yearned to show the strengths of their states through their designs.

Times have changed and so have state flags. Some have been redesigned. But others have remained the same for generations.

You aren't likely to see jet planes, computers, or rocket ships on a flag. They feature instead symbols of the past. Included are animals such as grizzly bears and pelicans. Or swords and caps that reflect old battles that brought freedom. Or mountains and rivers that show beauty. Every flag tells a different story.

Contents

Alabama

The simple crimson cross on a white background is similar to the famous Confederate battle flag. Alabama was among 11 states that fought for the Confederacy during the Civil War.

So ... Rectangle or Square?

State officials debated for years whether this flag should be shaped in a rectangle or square. A decision to maintain it as a rectangle was not made until 1987. The logic was that it had been reproduced in a rectangle for so long that it should not be changed.

State Motto:	Statehood Date:	Flag Adopted:
We Dare Defend Our Rights	December 14, 1819	1895

Alaska

This design was created for a contest in 1927 by 13-year-old John Bell Benson. The seven gold stars on the left represent the Big Dipper and the one on the right the North Star.

Quite a Competition!

Design contest winner John Bell Benson was born in Chignik, a small fishing village on the south shore of the Alaska Peninsula. He boasted an interesting background. His father was Swedish and his mother was Russian. The boy had to beat out 141 other kids that created designs for the Alaska flag. Most of the other designs are on display at the Alaska Historical Library and Museum.

State Motto:	Statehood Date:	Flag Adopted:
North to the Future	January 3, 1959	1927

Arizona

The setting sun that brings warmth and beauty to Arizona is brightly represented in its flag. So are the state colors of red and blue. The copper star honors a state that is the largest copper producer in America.

Color Commentary

Arizona gives tribute to the 13 original American colonies even though it became a state more than 100 years after they gained statehood. The yellow and red alternating stripes in this flag represent those colonies. Those colors also symbolize Spanish influence on Arizona.

State Motto:	Statehood Date:	Flag Adopted:
God Enriches	February 14, 1912	1917

Arkansas is the only state that produces diamonds. Hence the diamond in the middle of its flag. The 25 stars surrounding it explain that Arkansas was the 25th state admitted to the Union.

Honoring ... Michigan?

One of the two blue stars in the Arkansas flag honors the state of Michigan. Why? Because Arkansas and Michigan gained statehood around the same time. Michigan was the 26th state admitted to the union. Other stars within the diamond represent three influential countries in state history—the United States, France, and Spain.

State Motto:	Statehood Date:	Flag Adopted:
The People Rule	June 15, 1836	1924

A flag created to declare independence from Mexico in 1848 features a grizzly bear, which stands for strength. The lone star shows solidarity with Texas, which aided California in fighting for independence.

A Flag of Freedom

California settlers raised this flag at the Mexican stronghold in Sonoma after taking its commander prisoner. The flag declared the land as the "California Republic." But it was not adopted as the official state flag until more than 60 years later.

State Motto:	Statehood Date:	Flag Adopted:
Eureka!	September 9, 1850	1911

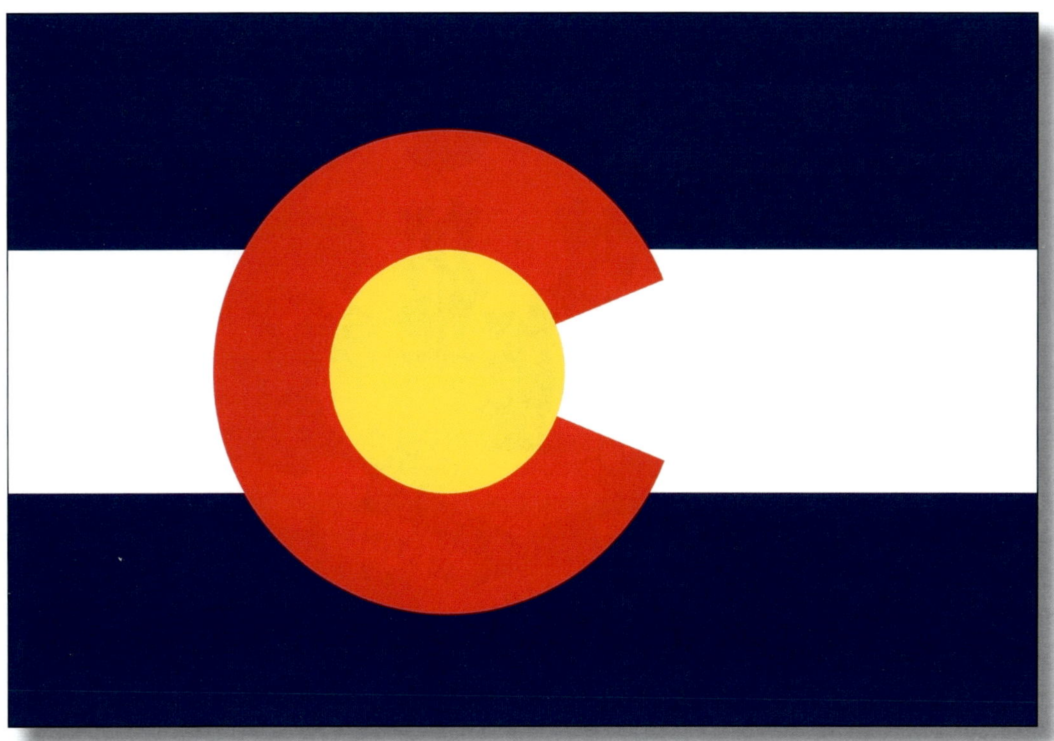

The different colors for different themes makes this flag interesting. Blue represents the clear skies of Colorado, white its snow-capped mountains, red the color of its earth, and gold its sunshine.

Confusion in Colorado

A patriotic organization known as the Daughters of the American Revolution (DAR) gave birth to this flag. Its members lamented in 1910 that Colorado had no state flag. They decided to have one created. Little did they know that a Colorado state flag had been sitting in a custodian's office since 1907. The DAR went ahead with its plan anyway and the flag it designed was adopted in 1911.

State Motto:	Statehood Date:	Flag Adopted:
Nothing Without the Deity	August 1, 1876	1911

Connecticut

The grapevines on the white shield represent religion, liberty, and knowledge. They also signify the original colonies of Hartford, Windsor, and Wethersfield.

Abby Day Gets Her Way

Abby Day was born in Connecticut, but raised in New Orleans. She married a Confederate captain, then moved back to Connecticut in 1888 after he died. She later learned to her disgust that her native state had no flag. She pestered state officials until they agreed to adopt one based on a Daughters of American Revolution design.

State Motto:	Statehood Date:	Flag Adopted:
He Who Is Transplanted Still Sustains	January 9, 1788	1897

A glance at this flag shows the date Delaware became the first of the United States. The diamond symbolizes founding father Thomas Jefferson referring to Delaware as a "jewel" along the Atlantic Ocean.

A Meaning for Every Symbol

Each image on the Delaware flag represents a strength of the state. The wheat and corn signify its agriculture. The ox shows the importance to the economy of raising animals. The blue water stands for the Delaware River, a hub of business and transportation. And the sailing ship represents the ship building industry of New Castle County.

State Motto:	Statehood Date:	Flag Adopted:
Liberty and Independence	December 7, 1787	1913

Pride in the heritage and beauty of Florida is prominent in its flag. The state seal in the middle shows a Seminole Indian, a steamboat, and a palm tree.

The Logic of Francis Fleming

The red cross in the center of the flag was suggested by Governor Francis Fleming and added in 1899. He reasoned that the plain white design looked like a surrender flag. He did not want that image to be conveyed as it flew atop a flagpole.

State Motto:	Statehood Date:	Flag Adopted:
In God We Trust	March 3, 1845	1895

Included in the 2003 redesign of this flag is a soldier representing defense of the United States Constitution. Also shown is the state motto: Wisdom, Justice, Moderation.

The 1956 Flag of Shame

Georgia has featured seven state flags. One adopted in 1956 featured an image of the Confederate battle flag from the Civil War. It was created in reaction to a Supreme Court ruling that southern states could no longer keep black children and white children in separate schools. Georgia lawmakers introducing the new flag stated a plan to close all public schools. They would then open them as private schools that could keep black students out.

State Motto:	Statehood Date:	Flag Adopted:
Wisdom, Justice, Moderation	January 2, 1788	2003

Hawaii

The last state admitted to the union boasts a flag within a flag. The Union Jack was the official flag of Hawaii long before the islands became part of the United States. From 1816 to 1959, it flew as the islands' national flag.

A Stripe for Every Island

The Hawaiian flag features eight horizontal stripes. They stand for the state's eight main islands. They are Hawaii, Kahoolawe, Kauai, Lanai, Maui, Molokai, Niihau, and Oahu. The capital and largest city in Hawaii is Honolulu. It sits on the island of Oahu, which is easily the most populous in the state.

State Motto:	Statehood Date:	Flag Adopted:
The Life of the Land Is Perpetuated in Righteousness	August 21, 1959	adopted 1816, modified 1845

Idaho

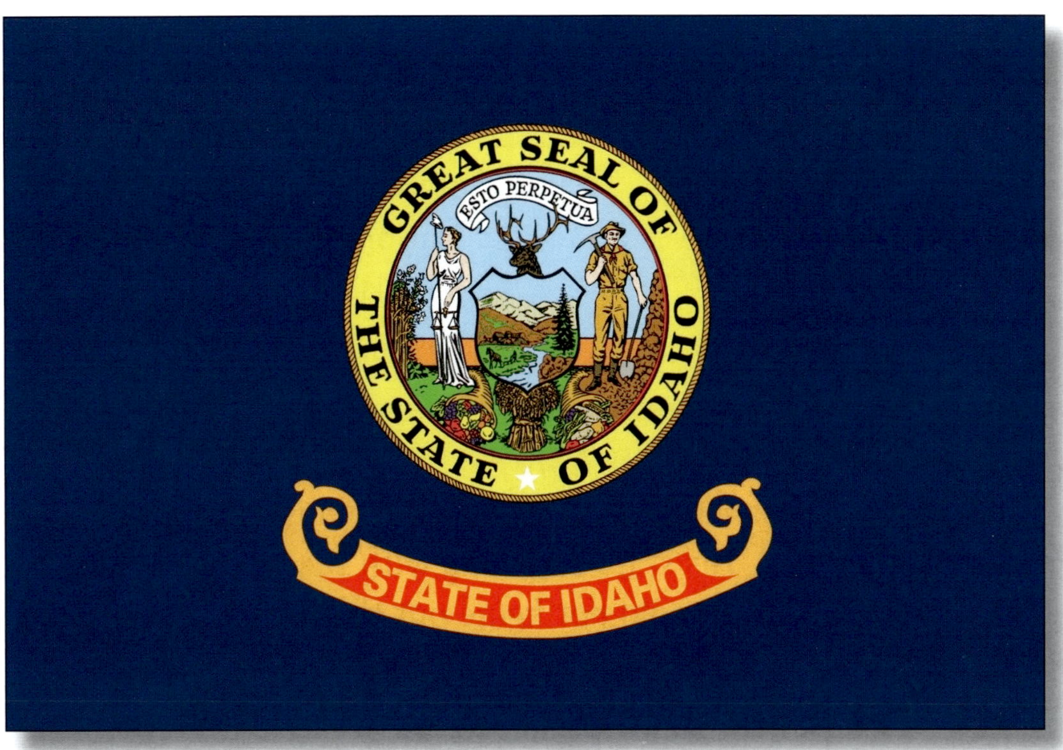

The only state seal designed by a woman features a miner and other symbols of Idaho. Emma Edwards expressed love for equality by displaying a male and female of similar height during a time when American women battled for voting rights.

Where is the Potato?

One would be mistaken to think a potato is highlighted on the Idaho flag. But it would be a logical mistake. Idaho is known for growing potatoes. It produces more potatoes than any state in the country. It has even adopted the potato as its state vegetable. But it is not featured in the state flag.

State Motto:	Statehood Date:	Flag Adopted:
Let It Be Perpetual	July 3, 1890	1957

Illinois

America's national bird dominates the Illinois flag. The bald eagle holds in its beak the state motto: State Sovereignty, National Union. That means Illinois embraces both freedom and unity with the United States.

Changing the Flag from Far Away

Soldier Bruce McDaniel of Illinois was serving his country during the Vietnam War in 1969. His state flag hung with the others on the mess hall wall. But his friends could not figure out the state it represented. McDaniel asked that the flag show the state name. His request was picked up by a state official. A new flag featuring the state name in large letters was soon adopted.

State Motto:	Statehood Date:	Flag Adopted:
State Sovereignty, National Union	December 3, 1818	1969

Indiana

Indiana was not one of the original 13 colonies, but they are honored by the outer stars on its flag. The torch represents liberty and learning. Its rays symbolize how those ideals have spread.

(Indiana continued)

Happy Birthday ... How About a Flag?

Indiana's 100th anniversary of statehood motivated a contest to design a state flag. The winner was Paul Hadley of Mooresville. He not only honored the 13 colonies with stars, but added five more stars in a semi-circle to honor the next five states admitted to the Union. Indiana, which was the 19th to be granted statehood, is represented by the star above the torch.

State Motto:	Statehood Date:	Flag Adopted:
Crossroads of America	December 11, 1816	1917

Iowa

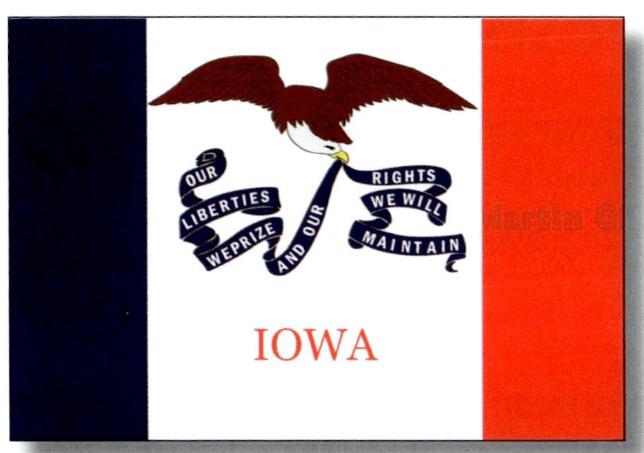

These colors match those in the flag of France, which played a major role in Iowa history. The white stripe honors Native Americans while the eagle symbolizes pride in the United States.

They Wanted One, They Got One

National Guard soldiers led the drive to adopt a state flag. They were stationed along the Mexican border during World War I. They suggested that a state flag was needed to identify their unit. That motivated Dixie Cornell Gebhart to design a flag in 1917. She was a member of the state's Daughters of the America Revolution organization.

State Motto:	Statehood Date:	Flag Adopted:
Our Liberties We Prize and Our Rights We Will Maintain	December 28, 1846	1921

A colorful emblem connects hard work to achievement. That ideal is captured in a motto exclaiming, "To the Stars Through Difficulty." The flag also shows the sunflower, which grows wild in Kansas.

In Other Words, Hard Work Pays Off

The state motto is displayed in Latin on the flag. The phrase "ad astra per astera" is translated as "to the stars through difficulty." It means that nothing worth doing can be achieved without effort. The motto serves to inspire the people of Kansas to work hard to fulfill their dreams.

State Motto:	Statehood Date:	Flag Adopted:
To the Stars Through Difficulty	January 29, 1861	1961

People allergic to goldenrod do not sneeze when they see two sprigs of the state flower on the Kentucky flag. The flag also depicts friendship between a pioneer and statesman. That represents the state motto shown within the seal.

From Lyrics to Motto

The state motto was taken from the lyrics of "The Liberty Song," a patriotic tune from the Revolutionary War. "United We Stand, Divided We Fall" is among the most famous state mottos in the country. It stresses the need for Kentuckians to stick together. The flag design came courtesy of Jesse Cox Burgess. He was an art teacher from the state capital of Frankfort.

State Motto:	Statehood Date:	Flag Adopted:
United We Stand, Divided We Fall	June 1, 1792	1918

Pelican pride motivated designers to feature one on the center of this flag. The state bird is shown feeding her young with drops of blood from her own body.

Make Up Your Mind!

Louisiana had flown 10 different flags before adopting this one in 1912. It flew the banners of Spain, France, and Great Britain before the United States purchased the Louisiana Territory in 1803. Louisiana even adopted the flag of an independent nation for two months after seceding from the Union as a Confederate state in 1861.

State Motto:	Statehood Date:	Flag Adopted:
Union, Justice, and Confidence	April 30, 1812	1912; revised in 2010

This unique flag features a farmer and seaman. They represent Maine's dependence on agriculture and the sea to produce food and jobs.

They are Fine with Pine

The first official flag for this state featured a blue North Star shining down on a pine tree. A new design greatly changed the flag eight years later. But the pine tree remained. A large one dominates the state seal in the middle of the flag. Underneath it rests a moose, which is the state animal.

State Motto:	Statehood Date:	Flag Adopted:
I Direct	March 15, 1820	1909

Maryland

This odd-looking flag is a tribute to tradition. The black-and-gold coat of arms is linked to Maryland founder George Calvert. The red-and-white one is tied to his mother's family, the Crosslands.

The Great Debate of Maryland

Is Maryland in the north or south? That question has been debated for years. And that debate has even been associated with its flag. Some Maryland citizens wore the red-and-white colors of the flag to show support for the South during the Civil War. But Maryland had not seceded from the Union like the other southern states. It did not officially fight for either side.

State Motto:	Statehood Date:	Flag Adopted:
Strong Deeds, Gentle Words	April 28, 1788	1904

Massachusetts

Massachusetts shows pride in its Native American heritage through its flag. The one centered on the shield was borrowed from an image on a colonial seal first displayed in 1639.

(Massachusetts continued)

A Flag of Peace and Liberty

The Algonquin Indian featured in the Massachusetts flag points his bow and arrow downward as a symbol of peace. The state motto also calls for peace, but not at the price of liberty. The desire to fight for liberty is represented above the shield by a bent arm holding a sword.

State Motto:	Statehood Date:	Flag Adopted:
By the Sword We Seek Peace, But Peace Only Under Liberty	February 5, 1788	1971

 # Michigan 

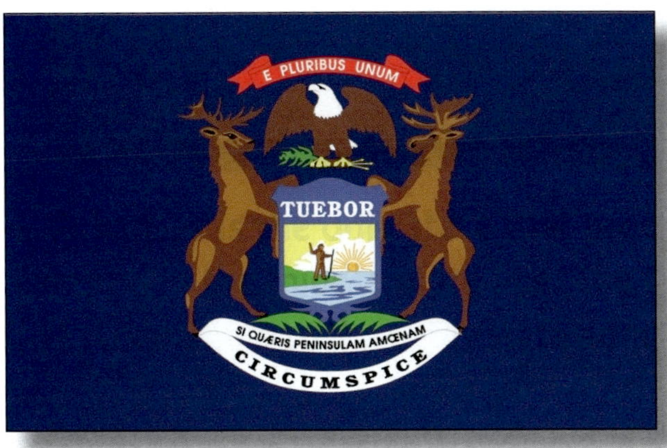

A man raising one arm in peace and holding a rifle in the other symbolizes a state embracing peace and the right to defend itself. The elk and moose are derived from the Hudson Bay Company coat of arms.

They Finally Found the Finest Flag

Michigan has embraced its state flag for more than 100 years. But it boasted two others before settling on the current design. The first featured a picture of Governor Stevens Thomson Mason on one side and the state coat of arms on the other. His image was replaced by the United States coat of arms in a flag adopted in 1865. That was the year Michigan and the other northern states won the Civil War.

State Motto:	Statehood Date:	Flag Adopted:
If You Seek a Peninsula, Look About You	January 26, 1837	1911

Minnesota

Three historic dates are displayed on this flag. The most prominent is 1858, when Minnesota gained statehood. The pine trees, ox, and stump symbolize its abundant forest resources.

Slipping Up on Lady's Slippers

The Minnesota flag required a change in 1957. That is when it was realized that it featured the wrong state flower. It had shown a wreath of a white flower called a "lady's slipper." The white lady's slipper is not native to Minnesota. The image was changed to that of a pink and white lady's slipper. That is the official state flower.

State Motto:	Statehood Date:	Flag Adopted:
The Star of the North	May 11, 1858	1957

Mississippi

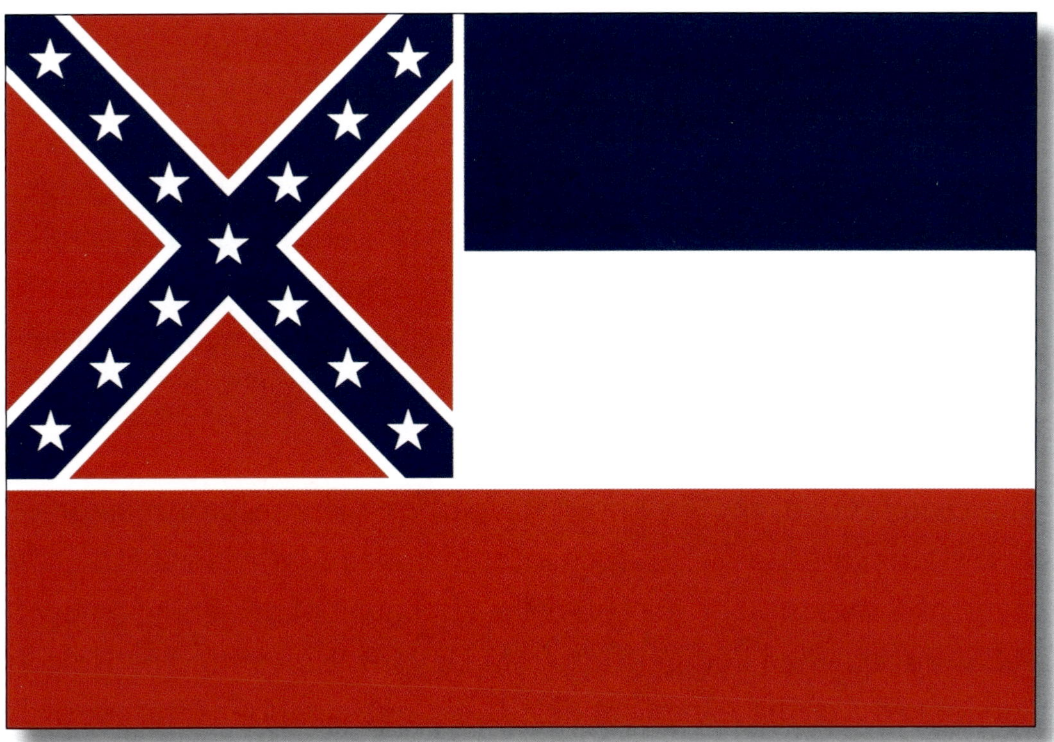

Heritage and national pride give meaning to the Mississippi flag. The stars in the upper left honor the 13 Confederate states. The red, white, and blue stripes represent the United States.

The Big Battle

The Confederate symbol from the Civil War shown on the upper left corner has been the center of heated debate for years. Some see it as a symbol of racism and hatred. After all, it reflects a time when Mississippi fought to maintain slavery. Others consider it a piece of history that should be maintained. Mississippi remains the only state to still display the Confederate symbol on its flag.

State Motto:	Statehood Date:	Flag Adopted:
By Valor and Arms	December 10, 1817	2001

The California flag shows one grizzly bear representing strength. The Missouri flag features three. The two large brown ones support a scroll that translated reads, "Let the welfare of the people be the supreme law."

Another 'Daughter' Came Through

The Daughters of the American Revolution were responsible for several state flags. Its Missouri chapter included Marie Elizabeth Oliver, the wife of a senator. She accepted the challenge of designing a new flag in 1908. But she had competition from Dr. N.R. Holcomb. The Holcomb design looked like the American flag. It did not symbolize Missouri. The Oliver flag was adopted instead in 1913.

State Motto:	Statehood Date:	Flag Adopted:
The Welfare of the People Shall Be the Supreme Law	August 10, 1821	1913

A pick and shovel in a colorful seal honors Montana miners who searched for gold and silver. The digging tools rest along the Great Falls of the Missouri River, which runs through the state.

(Montana continued)

Great Job, Colonel Kessler!

This flag came courtesy of Colonel Harry C. Kessler in 1898. Kessler served as head of a Montana volunteer army during the Spanish-American War. He yearned to create a flag that would distinguish his men from the forces of other states. Kessler designed one that would be adopted in 1905. A new flag that displayed the state name was accepted in 1981.

State Motto:	Statehood Date:	Flag Adopted:
Gold and Silver	November 8, 1889	1981

 # Nebraska 

This flag depicts hard work through images of a blacksmith and farmer's crops. A steamboat cruising the Missouri River and train speeding toward the Rocky Mountains depict Nebraska's place in the American heartland.

Don't Rag on the Nebraska Flag

It is against Nebraska law to insult the state flag. It is forbidden as well to use the flag as part of business advertising. State law also requires that it be displayed under or to the left of the American flag.

State Motto:	Statehood Date:	Flag Adopted:
Equality Before the Law	March 1, 1867	1963

Two sprigs of sagebrush, once used as food for cattle and medicine, display pride in the state flower. The silver and gold colors represent precious metals found in Nevada.

Rejected by the Governor

Only once has a proposed design for a Nevada state flag failed. That one was promoted by the cities of Elko, Reno, and Las Vegas in 1953. Their argument was that the existing flag was too expensive to produce at 20 dollars. The new one would cost just seven dollars and be affordable for Nevada organizations to display. But Governor Charles H. Russell rejected the design. He stated that the flag already in use captured a sense of dignity not found in the new one.

State Motto:	Statehood Date:	Flag Adopted:
All for Our Country	October 31, 1864	1991

Pride in the contribution of this state to American independence is reflected by the warship on the seal. The *USS Raleigh* built in New Hampshire was among the first 13 sent into battle during the Revolutionary War.

Taking it for Granite

New Hampshire is known as the Granite State. That explains the boulder of granite displayed within its state seal. That seal is surrounded by a laurel wreath that represents victory. The nine stars placed within the wreath symbolizes that New Hampshire was the ninth state admitted to the Union.

State Motto:	Statehood Date:	Flag Adopted:
Live Free or Die	June 21, 1788	1931

New Jersey

The symbolism of this flag includes images of the Roman Goddesses of Liberty and Agriculture. Above the shield sits a knight's helmet representing state independence and horse head denoting speed and strength.

A Great Coat of Arms, By George!

The color of the coat of arms featured in this flag can be traced back to George Washington. The American general directed that his Revolutionary War troops adopt a coat of arms of dark blue and yellowish-brown. Though the New Jersey flag has changed, the coat of arms colors has remained the same.

State Motto:	Statehood Date:	Flag Adopted:
Liberty and Prosperity	December 18, 1787	1896

(North Carolina continued)

The Declaration Date Debate

Did Mecklenburg County declare its independence from England on May 20, 1775? The state flag displays the date for that reason. Its citizens supposedly signed it upon learning of the Battle of Lexington, the first clash of the Revolutionary War. That was one year before the United States produced its famed Declaration of Independence. But no Mecklenburg Declaration was published until 1819. Even newspapers in 1775 made no reference to it.

State Motto:	Statehood Date:	Flag Adopted:
To Be, Rather Than to Seem	November 21, 1789	1991

 # North Dakota 

This flag was taken into battle by North Dakota soldiers in the late 1800s. Its American eagle carries an olive branch symbolizing peace and an arrow that represents liberty.

Still Wearing the Same Coat

The coat of arms displayed in the North Dakota flag closely resembles that of the United States. The similarity motivated an effort to change the flag in 1953. But the attempt failed. The state flag has remained the same since adoption in 1911.

State Motto:	Statehood Date:	Flag Adopted:
Liberty and Union Now and Forever, One and Inseparable	November 2, 1889	1911

Ohio

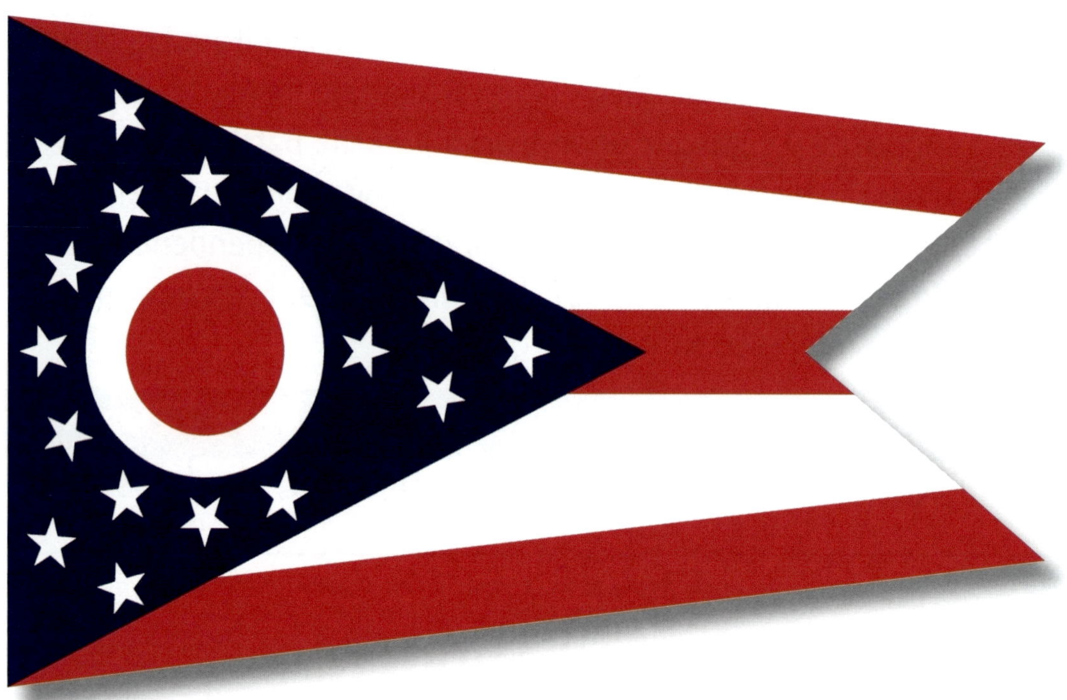

What is a burgee? It is the unusual shape of the only non-rectangular state flag. The blue triangle symbolizes Ohio's hills and valleys. The stripes denote its roads and waterways.

So ... Rectangle or Square?

Architect John Eisemann won a bid to design the Ohio building for the Pan-American Exposition in 1901. But he realized Ohio had no state flag. He set out to design one that would fly over the building. Eisemann yearned for it to be unique. The result was a shape unlike any other state flag in the country.

State Motto:	Statehood Date:	Flag Adopted:
With God All Things Are Possible	March 1, 1803	1902

Reminders of a rich Indian history dominate this flag. It shows a battle shield from the Osage tribe, the blue color of the Choctaw Indian battle flag, and a Native American peace pipe.

This Flag is a Fluke

A 1924 contest served to create a flag depicting unity between Native American and European American cultures. The winner was Louise Fluke, whose design featured a buffalo-skin shield with seven eagle feathers hanging from it. The shield includes an olive branch, a symbol of peace to Europeans.

State Motto:	Statehood Date:	Flag Adopted:
Labor Conquers All Things	November 16, 1907	2006

Oregon

Oregon boasts the only flag displaying designs on both sides. One shows a beaver, the state animal. The other displays an ox-drawn wagon, plow, and ax to honor the mining and farming of early settlers.

One Ship Coming, One Ship Going

The shield crest on the Oregon flag features an American eagle with two ships sailing the Pacific Ocean below it. The departing ship is British. The arriving ship is American. They symbolize trade between nations and the United States as an emerging world power.

State Motto:	Statehood Date:	Flag Adopted:
She Flies with Her Own Wings	February 14, 1859	1925

Pennsylvania

The horses flanking a coat of arms represent the power of Pennsylvania to thrive despite adversity. The ship represents trade, the plow symbolizes farming and the wheat denotes bountiful harvests.

(Pennsylvania continued)

The Same Blue

This flag boasts the same shade of blue shown on the American flag. That is no coincidence. Pennsylvania officials required that the colors match in 1907. The state flag has remained unchanged ever since.

State Motto:	Statehood Date:	Flag Adopted:
Virtue, Liberty, and Independence	December 12, 1787	1907

Rhode Island

The gold anchor centered in this flag depicts a shipping industry that allows many in Rhode Island to prosper. The 13 stars indicate the number of original American colonies. Rhode Island was the last of them to join the Union.

The Only 'Hope' of Solving the Mystery

Why is the word "Hope" displayed on this state seal and flag? Nobody seems to know. The best guess could be seen in a Rhode Island Historical Society publication from 1930. It claims that the words were likely inspired by the Biblical phrase "hope we have as an anchor of the soul." That phrase ties the word "hope" in with the anchor on the state flag.

State Motto:	Statehood Date:	Flag Adopted:
Hope	May 29, 1790	1897

South Carolina

What looks like a crescent moon displays instead the image on caps worn by South Carolina soldiers during the Revolutionary War. The palmetto tree defended those men against cannon balls fired by the British.

Another 'Revolutionary' Idea

The crescent moon and palmetto tree are not the only Revolutionary War references on the South Carolina flag. The dark blue also boasts significance. It is the same color of the uniforms worn by South Carolina soldiers in battle.

State Motto:	Statehood Date:	Flag Adopted:
While I Breathe I Hope – Prepared in Mind and Resources	May 23, 1788	1861

South Dakota

This small seal tells a big story. The plow and crops honor farmers and the steamboat represents trade and transportation. The beautiful Black Hills, sacred to the Sioux Indians, rise in the distance.

(South Dakota continued)

The Major Motto Switch

The first official flag of South Dakota featured the words "The Sunshine State" underneath a golden sun. But the motto was conceded to Florida in 1992. That is when South Dakota changed it to "The Mount Rushmore State." It is far better known for Mount Rushmore than for sunshine. Mount Rushmore is among the most famous landmarks in the United States. It is a sculpture of four legendary American presidents carved into the Black Hills.

State Motto:	Statehood Date:	Flag Adopted:
Under God the People Rule	November 2, 1889	1992

 # Tennessee 

Perhaps the simplest of state flags features three white stars. Its creator claimed that the stars denote the three different regions of the state: West, Middle, and East.

Wrong!

A magazine article in 1917 claimed the three stars signified that Tennessee was the third state admitted to the Union after the original 13. Flag designer LeRoy Stevens refuted it after the article was published. He added that the blue circle around the stars represents state unity.

State Motto:	Statehood Date:	Flag Adopted:
Agriculture and Commerce	June 1, 1796	1905

One can understand why the Lone Star State flag features a lone star. Its points signify five traits of outstanding Texas citizens. The red, white and blue colors represent (in order) bravery, purity and loyalty.

The Story of a Super-Sized State

Texas won a war of independence from Mexico in 1836. What was known as the Republic of Texas adopted its flag three years later. The United States angered Mexico by seeking to annex Texas into the Union. It was finally admitted in 1845. Its flag has remained the same for nearly 200 years, but was not officially adopted until 1933.

State Motto:	Statehood Date:	Flag Adopted:
Friendship	December 29, 1845	1933

It is no surprise that the Beehive State boasts a beehive in its flag. The honeybee symbolizes hard work and industry. Utah also honors the country with a bald eagle and American flag.

Two Dates with Destiny

The Utah flag features two dates. One is 1896, the year it became a state. The other is 1847. That is when settler and religious leader Brigham Young arrived in what became Salt Lake City, its capital and largest city. His followers practiced the Mormon religion. Utah still houses more Mormons than any other state.

State Motto:	Statehood Date:	Flag Adopted:
Industry	January 4, 1896	2011

Pride in Vermont's farms and beauty motivated a flag design featuring a cow, deer, wheat, mountains, forest, and pine tree. Pine boughs beneath the shield symbolize branches Vermont soldiers wore in hiding from the British during the War of 1812.

A Coat for Vermont

The folks of Vermont believed their flag looked too much like the American flag. They learned as they pushed for change in the early 1900s that their state flag had been rarely used anyway. But another flag carried by Vermont soldiers in three wars displayed the state coat of arms on a blue field. It was deemed to have stronger ties to Vermont. The result was that it became the official state flag in 1923.

State Motto:	Statehood Date:	Flag Adopted:
Freedom and Unity	March 4, 1791	1923

Virginia

This Revolutionary War era flag depicts the battle between good and evil. The good of Virginia and liberty are portrayed by the female Virtue. She stands in triumph over a soldier representing the tyranny of British rule.

A Sad Ending

The seal in the center of this flag was designed by George Wythe, who was among the original signers of the Declaration of Independence. In 1806, a relative was charged with poisoning Wythe, who died two weeks later.

State Motto:	Statehood Date:	Flag Adopted:
Thus Always to Tyrants	June 25, 1788	1950

Washington was named after the first American president. And George Washington is honored in its state flag, the only one to display a picture of a person or feature a green background.

A Jewel of a Seal

The seal featured on the Washington state flag was designed in 1889 by a jeweler from the capital city of Olympia. He used an ink bottle and silver dollar to draw its rings. He then pasted a postage stamp in the center for the picture of George Washington.

State Motto:	Statehood Date:	Flag Adopted:
Into the Future	November 11, 1889	1923

West Virginia

West Virginia adopted this state seal soon after breaking away from Confederate Virginia in 1863. The figures honor miners and farmers. Their rifles and caps depict the desire of West Virginians to fight for freedom.

The Birth of West Virginia

A vote in Virginia to join the Confederacy in 1861 led to the formation of West Virginia. Others in the state wanted to support the North in the Civil War. Residents in 39 western Virginia counties voted to remain in the United States. But the election results might have been tainted. Union troops camped at many of the polling places to keep Confederate voters out.

State Motto:	Statehood Date:	Flag Adopted:
Mountaineers are Always Free	June 20, 1863	1929

Workers of the water and land are honored by a flag featuring a sailor and miner. The shield highlights the state's main industries: navigation, mining, agriculture, and manufacturing.

That Makes Sense!

Wisconsin is known as the Badger State. The badger is the state animal. The University of Wisconsin mascot is the beaver. It is no wonder that the Wisconsin state flag features a beaver between its seal and motto.

State Motto:	Statehood Date:	Flag Adopted:
Forward	May 29, 1848	1981

Wyoming

This flag is rich with symbolism. The bison represents a vital source of food, clothing, and shelter to Native Americans. The woman celebrates the first state to allow females to vote. The bald eagle and shield depict patriotism. The men represent cattle ranching and mining.

The Bison, the Flag, and the Wind

Legend claims that Wyoming flag designer Verna Keays originally placed the bison facing its fly end. The bison was later reversed because they are known to weather the harsh Wyoming winters by facing the wind, which would blow in the opposite direction.

State Motto:	Statehood Date:	Flag Adopted:
Equal Rights	July 10, 1890	1917

Index

www.rourkeeducationalmedia.com

PHOTO CREDITS: Cover: Main cover photo © Png Studio Photography; Alabama Flag © Dolly Right; Alaska flag © dovla982; Arizona, Arkansas, Connecticut, Florida, Hawaii, Idaho, Illinois, Indiana, Kansas, Kentucky, Louisiana, Maine, Maryland, Michigan, Minnesota, Mississippi, Missouri, Nebraska, Nevada, New Hampshire, New Jersey, New Mexico, New York, North Carolina, North Dakota, Ohio, Oklahoma, Pennsylvania, Rhode Island, South Carolina, South Dakota, Tennessee, Texas, Utah, Vermont, Virginia, West Virginia, Wisconsin, Wyoming flags © Lukasz Stefanski; California flag © BOLDG; Colorado, Iowa, Montana flags © Svetocheck; Delaware flag © NaughtyNut; Georgia flag © PhotoRoman; Massachusetts, Washington flags © NAN SKYBLACK; Oregon flag © PhotoRoman. All images from Shutterstock.com

Edited by: Keli Sipperley   Cover and Interior design by: Nicola Stratford   www.nicolastratford.com

Library of Congress PCN Data

FLAGS / Martin Gitlin
(STATE GUIDES)
ISBN 978-1-68342-400-0 (hard cover)
ISBN 978-1-68342-470-3 (soft cover)
ISBN 978-1-68342-566-3 (e-Book)
Library of Congress Control Number: 2017931406

Rourke Educational Media
Printed in the United States of America, North Mankato, Minnesota